KEY QUESTIONS
in AMERICAN HISTORY



# WAS THE AMERICAN REVOLUTION REVOLUTIONARY?

KATLIN MURRAY

PowerKiDS
press
New York

Published in 2019 by The Rosen Publishing Group, Inc.
29 East 21st Street, New York, NY 10010



First Edition

Editor: Elizabeth Krajnik
Book Design: Tanya Dellaccio

Photo Credits: Cover (George Washington) Everett - Art/Shutterstock.com; cover (Washington crossing the Delaware) Fine Art/Corbis Historical/Getty Images; cover (Drafting of Declaration of Independence) https://commons.wikimedia.org/wiki/File:Declaration_of_Independence_(1819),_by_John_Trumbull.jpg; p. 5 PhotoQuest/Archive Photos/Getty Images; p. 7 (top) https://commons.wikimedia.org/wiki/File:George_Grenville_(1712%E2%80%931770)_by_William_Hoare_(1707-1792).jpg; p. 7 (bottom) https://commons.wikimedia.org/wiki/File:JohnLocke.png; pp. 9 (top), 13 DEA PICTURE LIBRARY/De Agostini/Getty Images; p. 9 (bottom) Historical/Corbis Historical/Getty Images; p. 10 Fotosearch/Archive Photos/Getty Images; p. 11 (top) Burstein Collection/Corbis Historical/Getty Images; p. 11 (bottom) https://commons.wikimedia.org/wiki/File:Official_Presidential_portrait_of_John_Adams_(by_John_Trumbull,_circa_1792).jpg; p. 15 (top) Archive Photos/Getty Images; p. 15 (bottom) Gilbert Carrasquillo/Moment Mobile/Getty Images; p. 17 (top) Print Collector/Hulton Archive/Getty Images; p. 17 (bottom) Sean Pavone/Shutterstock.com; p. 19 (top) https://commons.wikimedia.org/wiki/File:Map_of_the_Battle_of_Bunker_Hill_area.jpg; p. 19 (bottom) https://commons.wikimedia.org/wiki/File:Benedict_Arnold._Copy_of_engraving_by_H._B._Hall_after_John_Trumbull,_published_1879.,_1931_-_1932_-_NARA_-_532921.tif; p. 20 https://commons.wikimedia.org/wiki/File:United_States_Declaration_of_Independence.jpg; p. 21 (top) https://commons.wikimedia.org/wiki/File:Writing_the_Declaration_of_Independence_1776_cph.3g09904.jpg; p. 21 (bottom) https://commons.wikimedia.org/wiki/File:Grand-Union-Flag.jpg; p. 23 (top) https://commons.wikimedia.org/wiki/File:Surrender_of_General_Burgoyne.jpg; p. 23 (bottom) https://commons.wikimedia.org/wiki/File:BurgoyneByReynolds.jpg; p. 25 (top) https://commons.wikimedia.org/wiki/File:Surrender_of_Lord_Cornwallis.jpg; p. 25 (bottom) https://commons.wikimedia.org/wiki/File:First_Marquis_of_Cornwallis.jpg; p. 27 (top) https://commons.wikimedia.org/wiki/File:Treaty_of_Paris_1783_-_last_page_(hi-res).jpg; p. 27 (bottom) De Agostini/Biblioteca Ambrosiana/De Agostini Picture Library/Getty Images; p. 28 https://commons.wikimedia.org/wiki/File:Articles_page1.jpg; p. 29 https://commons.wikimedia.org/wiki/File:Articles_of_Confederation_1977_Issue-13c.jpg.

Library of Congress Cataloging-in-Publication Data

Names: Murray, Katlin, author.
Title: Was the American Revolution revolutionary? / Katlin Murray.
Description: New York : Power Kids Press, 2019. | Series: Key questions in American history | Includes index.
Identifiers: LCCN 2017058536| ISBN 9781508167624 (library bound) | ISBN 9781508167648 (pbk.) | ISBN 9781508167655 (6 pack)
Subjects: LCSH: United States–History–Revolution, 1775-1783–Juvenile literature.
Classification: LCC E208 .M984 2019 | DDC 973.3–dc23
LC record available at https://lccn.loc.gov/2017058536

Manufactured in the United States of America

CPSIA Compliance Information: Batch CS18PK: For Further Information contact Rosen Publishing, New York, New York at 1-800-237-9932

# CONTENTS

# ONE WAR LED TO ANOTHER

In many ways, the seeds of the American Revolution were planted when Great Britain won the French and Indian War (1754–1763). As a result of that victory, Great Britain took over much of France and Spain's territory in North America. Now that the American colonists didn't have to worry about as many enemies nearby, many realized their connection to the British king and his **Parliament** was very weak.

Great Britain began taxing the colonists to help pay to defend the territories Britain had gained. The colonists felt that these taxes were unfair, which led to conflict between them and the British crown.

Eventually, this conflict led to the American **Revolution** (1775–1783) and the colonies gained independence from Great Britain. The birth of a new nation made the American Revolution revolutionary.

THIS ILLUSTRATION SHOWS GEORGE WASHINGTON FIGHTING DURING THE FRENCH AND INDIAN WAR. THIS WAR BETWEEN GREAT BRITAIN, FRANCE, AND THEIR NATIVE AMERICAN ALLIES CHANGED THE BORDERS WITHIN NORTH AMERICA.

# SUGAR ACT

After the French and Indian War ended, Great Britain needed a way to fund its new territories. The government decided to create new taxes on the colonists to pay for **infrastructure** and defense. Until this point, Great Britain hadn't paid much attention to the North American colonies. The colonists weren't used to interference or taxes from any government except for the colonial governments.

The Sugar Act, put in place in 1764, allowed the British government to collect taxes on sugar and a sugar product called molasses coming into the colonies from non-British sources. Although the colonists didn't agree with this act, they accepted it anyway. The British government created a court in Halifax, Nova Scotia, to try those who didn't follow the rules of the Sugar Act.

GEORGE GRENVILLE WAS PRIME MINISTER OF GREAT BRITAIN FROM 1763 TO 1765. THE TAXES HE PUT INTO PLACE WHILE IN OFFICE CAUSED TENSION BETWEEN BRITAIN AND THE COLONIES.

GEORGE GRENVILLE

JOHN LOCKE

### HISTORIC MOMENTS

English **philosopher** John Locke thought the government had a duty to create laws that protected citizens' right to life, liberty, and property. His ideas affected the Founding Fathers as they wrote the Declaration of Independence.

## STAMP ACT

A year later, the British government put the Stamp Act in place. The Stamp Act was a way for the government to make money by taxing paper items such as newspapers and cards, as well as dice. A stamp on the paper showed the tax had been paid. This was the first direct tax on the colonists. A direct tax is one that's imposed directly on the taxpayers. Previous taxes had been collected on imported goods. The colonists tended to see those taxes as benefiting the entire empire rather than simply making money for it.

Many of the colonists thought the Stamp Act was unfair. They became angry and began to **rebel** against the British government. They held **riots**, burned stamps, and frightened stamp **distributors**. In 1766, Parliament repealed, or did away with, the act.

**THIS CARTOON SHOWS A FUNERAL PROCESSION FOR THE STAMP ACT ON THE RIVER THAMES IN LONDON, ENGLAND. MR. GEORGE STAMP CARRIES THE COFFIN OF MISS AMERIC STAMP. BEHIND THE FUNERAL PROCESSION IS A CRATE MARKED "STAMPS FROM AMERICA."**

**STAMP ACT RIOT**

# BOSTON MASSACRE

Soon, however, Parliament added new taxes on imported goods. Colonists continued to resist these taxes. British leaders in the colonies asked Parliament to send soldiers to protect them. In October 1768, British soldiers arrived in the colonies, but their presence caused tensions to rise.

After a series of confrontations between British troops and colonists, the two groups clashed on March 5, 1770, in Boston, Massachusetts. Colonists attacked British soldiers by throwing snow, ice, and oyster shells at them. One soldier shot his gun out of fear, which signaled to the other soldiers that it was OK to shoot. Three people died during the attack and two people died later from their wounds. This event became known as the Boston **Massacre**.

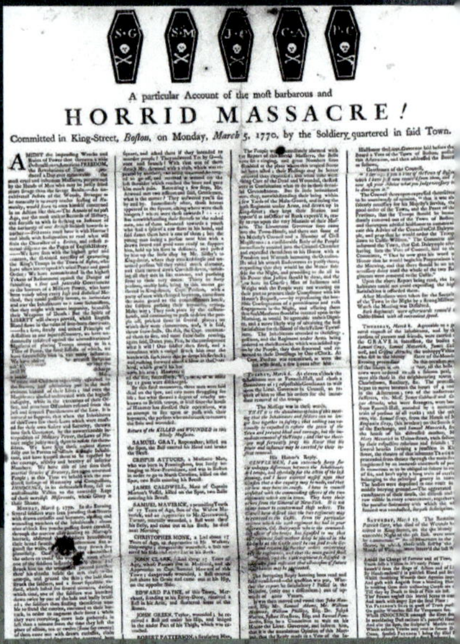

A particular Account of the most barbarous and

HORRID MASSACRE!

Committed in King-Street, *Boston*, on Monday, *March* 5, 1770, by the Soldiery quartered in said Town.

British Captain Thomas Preston and eight of his men were arrested, but they were later released.

THIS WELL-KNOWN IMAGE, WHICH DEPICTS BRITISH SOLDIERS STANDING IN A LINE SHOOTING INNOCENT PEOPLE, IS AN INACCURATE REPRESENTATION OF WHAT HAPPENED IN THE BOSTON MASSACRE.

## THE AFTERMATH

After the Boston Massacre, many troops left Boston, as did customs agents. Each side blamed the other, with several people writing accounts of what happened. Captain Preston wrote a personal account from his prison cell. This account was published in London's *Public Advertiser* in April 1770. John Adams, who would later help found the United States of America and become the second president of the United States, helped defend the British soldiers in court.

JOHN ADAMS

# BOSTON TEA PARTY

In 1773, British Parliament passed the Tea Act, which was created to help the East India Company, a British trading company, make more money. The company was struggling financially.

The Tea Act gave the East India Company a **monopoly** on all the tea going to the colonies, which allowed it to sell tea at the cheapest price available there. This angered many of the merchants in Boston, who joined with other **patriots** to protest the Tea Act and the company's monopoly.

On the evening of December 16, 1773, about 60 men disguised themselves as Native Americans and snuck onto the ships in Boston Harbor. They dumped 342 chests of tea into the water. As punishment, Parliament passed the Intolerable Acts, which included the Boston Port Bill. This bill stopped trade with Boston until the colonists paid back the value of the tea.

**PATRIOTS CLIMBED ABOARD THE *DARTMOUTH, ELEANOR,* AND *BEAVER* TO DUMP TEA AND PROTEST BRITISH CONTROL. TODAY, PEOPLE REENACT THE BOSTON TEA PARTY TO CELEBRATE THE PATRIOTS' FIGHT FOR THE COLONISTS' RIGHTS.**

### QUARTERING ACT

After the French and Indian War, Great Britain decided to keep soldiers in the colonies to keep costs low. Parliament achieved this by passing the Quartering Act in 1765. The Quartering Act also became a way for Parliament to show that it had power over the colonists. The act required colonists to provide British soldiers staying in their towns with food, drink, housing, and transportation. The fourth part of the Intolerable Acts included new rules about housing British soldiers. The Intolerable Acts made the colonists even more determined to fight back.

# FIRST CONTINENTAL CONGRESS

After the passage of the Intolerable Acts in spring 1774, tensions between the colonists and British authorities grew. As a result, 56 representatives from 12 of the 13 colonies—all except Georgia—met on September 5, 1774, at Carpenter's Hall in Philadelphia, Pennsylvania. These men met in secret to discuss the colonists' concerns. They created a declaration of personal rights, which stated they would remain loyal to the British crown but their rights must be protected.

The Continental Congress also passed the Articles of Association, which called for a **boycott** on goods imported from Britain. This boycott was to begin December 1, 1774, if the Intolerable Acts were not repealed. By September 10, 1775, the colonies would stop exporting goods as well. Great Britain didn't repeal the acts. By April 1775, however, the boycott no longer mattered.

THIS IMAGE SHOWS GEORGE WASHINGTON, PATRICK HENRY, AND EDMUND PENDLETON ON THEIR WAY TO THE FIRST CONTINENTAL CONGRESS.

CARPENTER'S HALL

### HISTORIC MOMENTS

Parts of the Articles of Association included a ban on the slave trade, cutting off economic ties to Great Britain, and a promise colonial products would remain affordable for the colonists.

# BATTLES OF LEXINGTON AND CONCORD

The battles of Lexington and Concord marked the first real combat between British soldiers and colonial patriots. In response to a command by Parliament, British General Thomas Gage ordered his troops to take away a store of the colonists' weapons, which were located in Concord, Massachusetts.

Gage's men marched from Boston. On the morning of April 19, 1775, 77 minutemen met Gage's 700 men in Lexington, Massachusetts. The minutemen knew the British troops were on their way because other colonists warned them. Historians don't know which group shot first, but fighting at Lexington resulted in eight minutemen dead and nine wounded. Only one British soldier was injured.

The British regrouped and moved on to Concord, where the colonists had hidden or destroyed most of their weapons. Hundreds of minutemen met the British there. The British eventually retreated to Boston. The colonial soldiers fired at them along the way.

**THE BATTLES OF LEXINGTON AND CONCORD MARKED THE BEGINNING OF THE AMERICAN REVOLUTION.**

## HISTORIC MOMENTS

Colonial soldiers were called minutemen because they promised to be ready to fight with only a minute's notice. These men were often untrained.

## PAUL REVERE

Paul Revere was an outspoken supporter of the patriot cause. He took part in the Boston Tea Party and rode from Boston to Concord on the night of April 16, 1775, to warn the patriots about the British. Two nights later, Revere and William Dawes rode from Charlestown to Lexington to warn patriot leaders John Hancock and Samuel Adams to flee because British troops were searching for them. Revere arranged to have lanterns set up in Boston's Old North Church to warn the colonists of the British arrival.

# WASHINGTON TAKES CONTROL

After the battles of Lexington and Concord, the colonies and Great Britain got ready for more. The Continental Congress made many decisions for the colonists, including preparing for defense, readying soldiers, and making George Washington the leader of the military.

On July 3, 1775, Washington took control of the colonial forces. He began to recruit more troops as fighting continued around Massachusetts and New York. Meanwhile, some American troops moved to attack Canada. One group of soldiers captured Montreal while another group led by Benedict Arnold tried unsuccessfully to take Quebec. The British won and the Americans retreated to Fort Ticonderoga in New York State.

Fighting in the South was more fruitful for the patriots. In June 1776, the British failed to take Charleston, South Carolina. This battle refocused the fighting to the North.

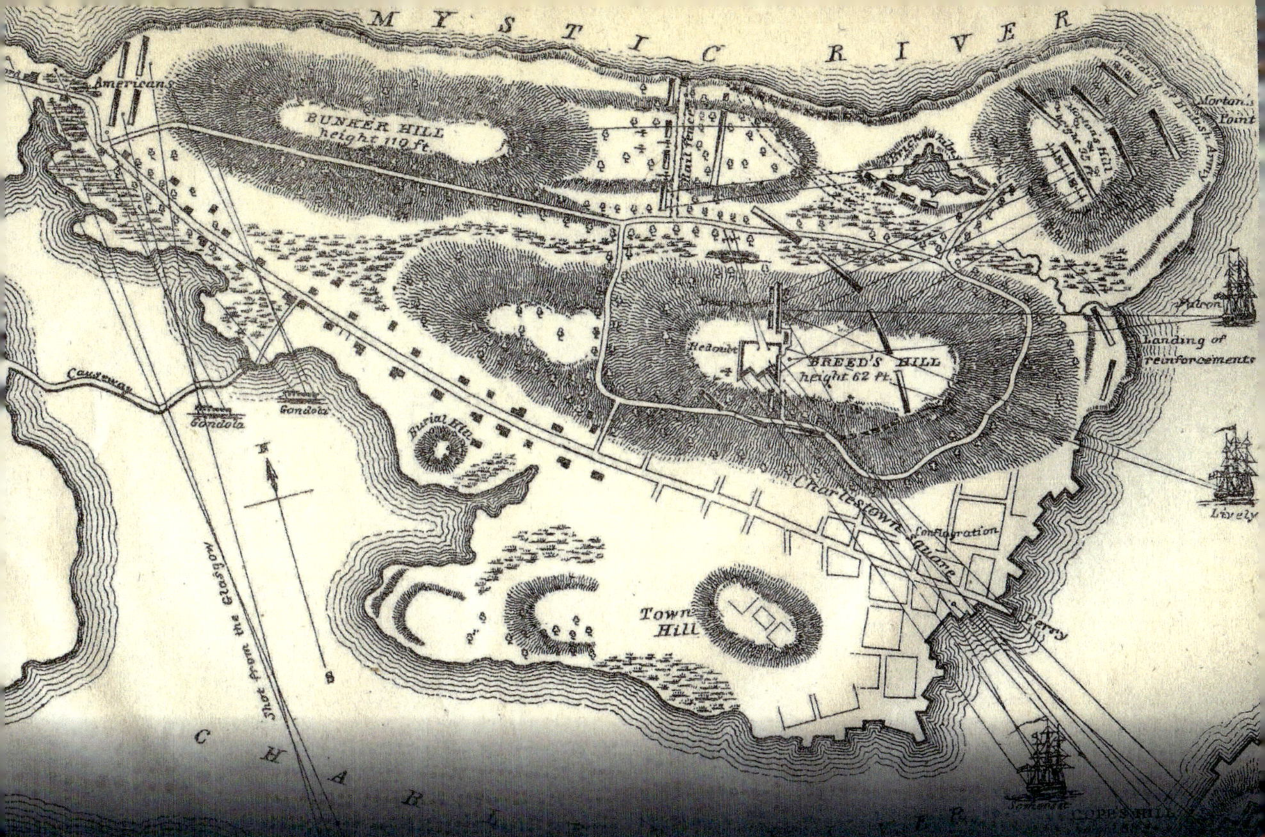


**GEORGE WASHINGTON WAS APPOINTED TO COMMAND THE AMERICAN FORCES JUST BEFORE THE BATTLE OF BUNKER HILL TOOK PLACE.**

## HISTORIC MOMENTS

Benedict Arnold fought on the patriots' side until 1779, when he switched sides to fight for the British. Today, many people know his name without realizing his place in history.

# DECLARATION OF INDEPENDENCE

The Continental Congress continued to meet, but now it was working toward independence. In December 1775, the congress told Parliament that it had no authority over the colonies. In May 1776, it recommended the colonies create their own governments.

On June 11, 1776, congressional leaders chose a group of men, including John Adams and Benjamin Franklin, to **draft** a statement explaining why the colonies were declaring independence. The group asked Thomas Jefferson to write the first draft.

On July 2, representatives met at the Pennsylvania State House in Philadelphia (now known as Independence Hall) to vote on a resolution of independence. Two days after that, they approved the written Declaration of Independence. However, they didn't sign it until August 2 or later.

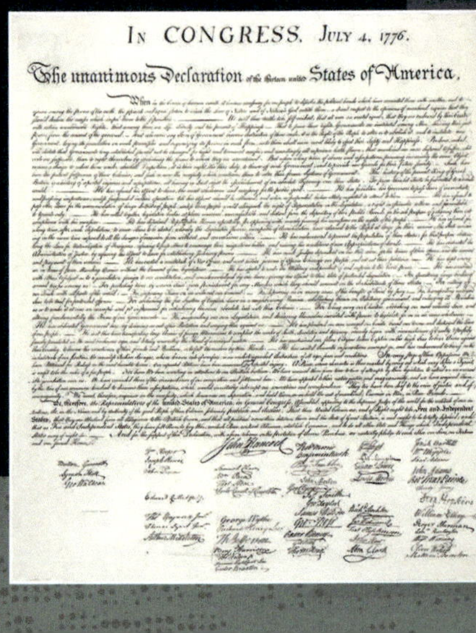

IN CONGRESS, JULY 4, 1776.

The unanimous Declaration of the ... States of America,

**TODAY, PEOPLE CAN VIEW THE ORIGINAL DECLARATION OF INDEPENDENCE AT THE NATIONAL ARCHIVES IN WASHINGTON, D.C.**

### THE AMERICAN FLAG

The first national flag, sometimes known as the Continental Colours, was raised January 1, 1776, at Prospect Hill in Charlestown, Massachusetts, at the request of General George Washington. It had 13 horizontal red and white stripes and a small British flag in the upper left corner. This flag was flown on a number of occasions and for a number of reasons. The flag we know as the first official national flag wasn't approved until June 14, 1777.

# THE FIGHTING CONTINUES

After the colonies officially declared independence from Great Britain, British and American forces continued to clash. The British wanted to divide New England and the other states.

British general John Burgoyne and his army marched south from Canada to gain control of New York. He won a small battle at Ticonderoga on July 5, 1777, and continued to move south. The Americans defeated a number of his German allies on August 16. American forces led by General Horatio Gates caused much damage to Burgoyne's army at the Battle of Freeman's Farm in New York on September 19 and defeated it at Bemis Heights on October 7. Burgoyne surrendered at Saratoga on October 17, 1777.

France had secretly been giving the colonies money and supplies since 1776. After the Battles of Saratoga, the French began readying troops. France officially declared war in June 1778.

GENERAL BURGOYNE'S SURRENDER AT SARATOGA PREVENTED THE BRITISH FROM SEPARATING NEW ENGLAND FROM THE REST OF THE COUNTRY.

JOHN BURGOYNE

## HISTORIC MOMENTS

Women played an important role as spies for both sides during the American Revolution. They would listen to other people's conversations about military movements and pass this information on.

# BRITISH SURRENDER AT YORKTOWN

The final major battle of the American Revolution began in mid-September 1781. British General Charles Cornwallis had been building a base at Yorktown, Virginia, since August. After hearing that the French had arrived in Chesapeake Bay with ships and 3,000 soldiers, General George Washington and 2,500 soldiers and the French General Jean-Baptiste de Vimeur, comte de Rochambeau, with his 4,000 soldiers moved south to Virginia.

Cornwallis expected aid from the British navy, but it never arrived because the French navy blocked the ships. The combined American and French forces arrived in Yorktown and surrounded the city September 28. For the next two weeks, the French and American forces fired on the city and Cornwallis's troops. He surrendered on October 19, 1781.

Even though there were still British soldiers throughout the colonies, the surrender at Yorktown ended fighting on land in the Revolutionary War.

GENERAL CORNWALLIS DIDN'T GO TO THE SURRENDER CEREMONY. INSTEAD, HE SENT GENERAL CHARLES O'HARA, PICTURED HERE WITH AMERICAN GENERAL BENJAMIN LINCOLN.

CHARLES CORNWALLIS

# PEACE OF PARIS

Peace agreements between Great Britain and the United States began with an early treaty signed on November 30, 1782, in Paris by Great Britain and the United States.

On September 3, 1783, representatives of Britain and the United States signed the official Treaty of Paris, which officially ended the American Revolution and recognized American independence. Britain also signed treaties with France, Spain, and the Netherlands.

Britain surrendered the land between the Allegheny Mountains and the Mississippi River to the United States but kept control of Canada. The Treaty of Paris gave Americans access to fishing grounds in Newfoundland. It also granted both Great Britain and the United States the ability to travel on the Mississippi River. The Continental Congress promised to tell the states to treat Loyalists, Americans who'd sided with the British, fairly.

# TREATY OF PARIS

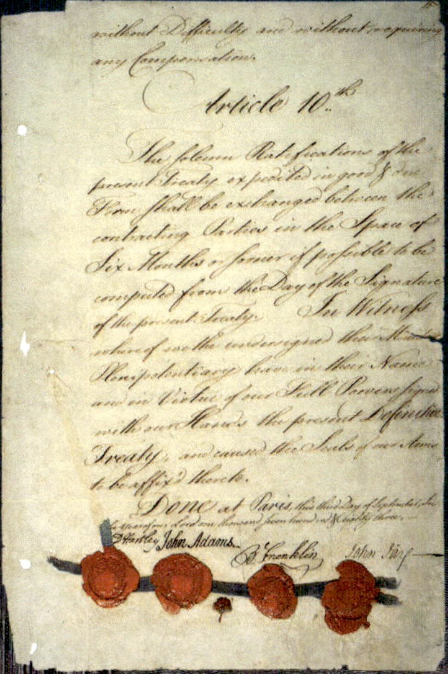

without Difficulty and without requiring any Compensation.

Article 10th.

The solemn Ratifications of the present Treaty expedited in good & due Form shall be exchanged between the contracting Parties in the Space of Six Months or sooner if possible to be computed from the Day of the Signature of the present Treaty. In Witness whereof we the undersigned their Ministers Plenipotentiary have in their Name and in Virtue of our Full Powers signed with our Hands the present Definitive Treaty, and caused the Seals of our Arms to be affixed thereto.

Done at Paris

Hartley John Adams. B Franklin John Jay

THIS IMAGE SHOWS THE SIGNING OF THE TREATY OF PARIS IN 1783. JOHN JAY AND BENJAMIN FRANKLIN ARE STANDING AT THE LEFT.

# WAS IT REVOLUTIONARY?

The American Revolution was, without a doubt, revolutionary. The colonists overthrew British authority in the colonies, declared their independence, and created their own federal and state governments. It was revolutionary because it brought about great change and paved the way for other colonies to declare their independence or overthrow a monarchy. One of the revolutions that followed was the French Revolution of 1789.

One of the most revolutionary things about the American Revolution is that it ended with the birth of a new country—and the adoption of a different form of government by that nation. Rather than a monarchy, the leaders of the new United States chose to make the young nation a democracy, or a country in which the people elect the government. That was very revolutionary!

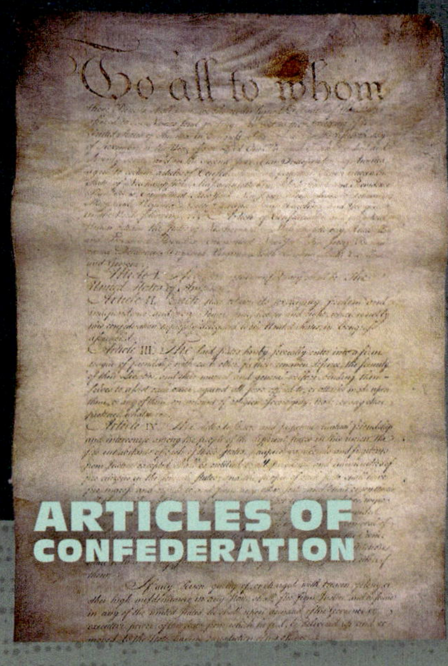


ARTICLES OF CONFEDERATION

**THE ARTICLES OF CONFEDERATION, THE FIRST CONSTITUTION OF THE UNITED STATES, WAS IN PLACE FROM 1781 TO 1789. IT WAS REPLACED BY THE U.S. CONSTITUTION ON MARCH 4, 1789.**

## CAUSES OF THE FRENCH REVOLUTION

The French Revolution had a number of causes. A class of wealthy French commoners called the bourgeoisie arose in the 1700s. They wanted a share of the political power. Also, in the 18th century, Europe's population grew very quickly. France's population was especially large. A group of educated thinkers known as the philosophes voiced their opinions on economic issues caused by this growth. France's participation in the American Revolution cost the country a great deal of money. The French monarchy became overwhelmed by these issues, and the people started the revolution, which is also called the Revolution of 1789.

# TIMELINE

**1754–1763**

France, Great Britain, and their allies fight in the French and Indian War.

**1764**

British Parliament passes the Sugar Act as a means to make money by taxing sugar and molasses imported to the colonies from non-British sources.

**1765**

Parliament passes the Stamp Act, a direct tax on paper items in the American colonies.

**1776**

Parliament repeals the Stamp Act.

**MARCH 5, 1770**

A conflict between colonists and British soldiers results in the death of five people. This is called the Boston Massacre.

**1773**

Parliament passes the Tea Act, which gives the East India Company a monopoly on tea going into the colonies.

**DECEMBER 16, 1773**

The Boston Tea Party takes place in Boston Harbor.

**1774**

Parliament passes the Intolerable Acts as a way to punish the colonists for acting out against British authority.

**SEPTEMBER 5, 1774**

The First Continental Congress meets in Philadelphia, Pennsylvania.

**APRIL 19, 1775**

British troops marching from Boston are met by colonial minutemen, leading to the Battles of Lexington and Concord and marking the official beginning of the American Revolution.

**JULY 4, 1776**

The Continental Congress approves the Declaration of Independence.

**OCTOBER 19, 1781**

General Charles Cornwallis surrenders to American forces at Yorktown.

**SEPTEMBER 3, 1783**

Representatives of the United States and Great Britain sign the Treaty of Paris, marking the end of the American Revolution and recognizing the United States as an independent country.

# GLOSSARY

**ally:** A person or country associated with another for a common purpose.

**archive:** A place in which public records or historical papers are saved.

**boycott:** A refusal to buy, use, or participate in something.

**distributor:** A person or company that distributes, or deals out, something.

**draft:** To create a draft, or a piece of writing, for the first time.

**infrastructure:** The equipment and structures needed for a country, state, or region to function properly.

**massacre:** The violent killing of many people.

**monopoly:** Complete control of the entire supply of goods or of a service in a certain area or market.

**Parliament:** The British lawmaking body.

**patriot:** A person who loves his or her country and strongly supports it.

**philosopher:** A person who tries to discover and to understand the basic nature of knowledge.

**rebel:** To fight against authority.

**revolution:** The overthrow of a ruler or government by violent action. Also, a sudden, extreme, or complete change.

**riot:** A violent public disturbance by a group of people.

# INDEX



# WEBSITES

Due to the changing nature of Internet links, PowerKids Press has developed an online list of websites related to the subject of this book. This site is updated regularly. Please use this link to access the list: www.powerkidslinks.com/kqah/amrev